麦格希 中英双语阅读文库

最受欢迎的世界名著故事
第1辑

【美】马克·吐温　【西】塞万提斯●著

刘慧●译

麦格希中英双语阅读文库编委会●编

全国百佳图书出版单位
吉林出版集团股份有限公司

图书在版编目（CIP）数据

最受欢迎的世界名著故事. 第1辑 /（美）马克·吐温,
(西) 塞万提斯著；麦格希中英双语阅读文库编委会编；
刘慧译. -- 2版. -- 长春：吉林出版集团股份有限公司,
2018.3（2022.1重印）
（麦格希中英双语阅读文库）
ISBN 978-7-5581-4781-4

Ⅰ.①最… Ⅱ.①马… ②塞… ③麦… ④刘… Ⅲ.
①英语—汉语—对照读物②故事—作品集—美国—现代
Ⅳ.①H319.4：I

中国版本图书馆CIP数据核字(2018)第046630号

最受欢迎的世界名著故事　第1辑

编	麦格希中英双语阅读文库编委会	
插　画：	齐　航　李延霞	
责任编辑：	沈丽娟	
封面设计：	冯冯翼	
开　本：	660mm×960mm　1/16	
字　数：	180千字	
印　张：	10	
版　次：	2018年3月第2版	
印　次：	2022年1月第2次印刷	

出　版：	吉林出版集团股份有限公司
发　行：	吉林出版集团外语教育有限公司
地　址：	长春市福祉大路5788号龙腾国际大厦B座7层
电　话：	总编办：0431-81629929
	发行部：0431-81629927　0431-81629921(Fax)
印　刷：	北京一鑫印务有限责任公司

ISBN 978-7-5581-4781-4　定价：36.00元

前言 *PREFACE*

英国思想家培根说过：阅读使人深刻。阅读的真正目的是获取信息，开拓视野和陶冶情操。从语言学习的角度来说，学习语言若没有大量阅读就如隔靴搔痒，因为阅读中的语言是最丰富、最灵活、最具表现力、最符合生活情景的，同时读物中的情节、故事引人入胜，进而能充分调动读者的阅读兴趣，培养读者的文学修养，至此，语言的学习水到渠成。

"麦格希中英双语阅读文库"在世界范围内选材，涉及科普、社会文化、文学名著、传奇故事、成长励志等多个系列，充分满足英语学习者课外阅读之所需，在阅读中学习英语、提高能力。

◎难度适中

本套图书充分照顾读者的英语学习阶段和水平，从读者的阅读兴趣出发，以难易适中的英语语言为立足点，选材精心、编排合理。

◎精品荟萃

本套图书注重经典阅读与实用阅读并举。既包含国内外脍炙人口、耳熟能详的美文，又包含科普、人文、故事、励志类等多学科的精彩文章。

◎功能实用

本套图书充分体现了双语阅读的功能和优势，充分考虑到读者课外阅读的方便，超出核心词表的词汇均出现在使其意义明显的语境之中，并标注释义。

鉴于编者水平有限，凡不周之处，谬误之处，皆欢迎批评教正。

我们真心地希望本套图书承载的文化知识和英语阅读的策略对提高读者的英语著作欣赏水平和英语运用能力有所裨益。

丛书编委会

Contents

The Adventures of Tom Sawyer

汤姆·索亚历险记

A Naughty Boy Tom Sawyer | naughty *adj.* 淘气的

"Tom, Tom, where are you?"

Aunt Polly looked under the bed.

As she did, a small boy jumped out of the closet. | closet *n.* 壁橱

"What were you doing in there?" asked Aunt Polly.

"Nothing, Aunt," answered Tom.

"You were eating jam again, weren't | jam *n.* 果酱

淘气包汤姆·索亚

"汤姆，汤姆，你在哪儿？"

波莉姨妈看了看床底下。

她往床下看的时候，一个小男孩从壁橱里跳了出来。

"你在那里面干吗？"波莉姨妈问。

"没什么，姨妈。"汤姆回答。

"你又在偷吃果酱，对不对？"波莉姨妈说。

you?" said Aunt Polly.

"Oh, look behind you, Aunt," said Tom.

Aunt Polly turned around, but there was nothing behind her.

turn around 转身

When she turned back, she saw Tom running away.

run away 逃跑

"That boy knows too many tricks," she laughed.

trick *n.* 花招；诡计

Tom didn't go to school that afternoon.

"哦，看你身后，姨妈。"汤姆说。

波莉姨妈转过身，但是后面什么也没有。

等她转回身，却看见汤姆一溜烟跑掉了。

"那孩子花招真多。"她笑起来。

那天下午汤姆没有去上学。

Instead, he went swimming and played with his friends.

instead *adv.* 相反地

He and his friends pretended to be pirates.

pretend *v.* 假扮

pirate *n.* 海盗

They chased each other through the long grass, in the mud and up the trees.

When Tom returned home, his clothes were very dirty.

"Tom, what a mess!" cried Aunt Polly.

mess *n.* 脏乱

~~~~~~

相反，他跑去游了会儿泳，又和朋友们玩闹了一场。

他和朋友们假扮海盗。

他们互相追逐，一会儿跑到高高的草丛里，一会儿跑到泥地上，一会儿又爬上了树。

汤姆回家的时候，衣服脏得一塌糊涂。

"汤姆，怎么弄得这么脏！"波莉姨妈叫起来。

"You didn't go to school today. I'll punish you. You must paint the garden fence tomorrow," said Aunt Polly angrily.

The next day was very hot.

Tom looked at the fence and sighed, "Oh, this is terrible. The fence is so big."

Just then, one of Tom's friends, Ben, came around the corner.

Tom had a wonderful idea and began

punish *v.* 惩罚

paint *v.* 给……上油漆

fence *n.* 篱笆

sigh *v.* 叹气

wonderful *adj.* 绝妙的

"你今天没去上学，我要罚你。明天你得去给花园的篱笆刷油漆。"波莉姨妈生气地说。

第二天天气非常热。

汤姆看着篱笆直叹气："唉，这太糟糕了。篱笆这么长。"

就在这时，汤姆的一个朋友，本，从街角转过来。

汤姆想到一个绝妙的主意，开始动手给篱笆刷漆。

painting the fence.

"What are you doing?" asked Ben.

"I'm painting this fence. It is a lot of fun," answered Tom.

fun *n.* 乐趣

"Can I paint the fence?" asked Ben.

"Well, okay, but you have to give me something," answered Tom.

"All I have is this dead cat," said Ben.

dead *adj.* 死亡的

Tom took the dead cat and gave Ben a

"你在干吗?"本问。

"我在给篱笆刷油漆。非常好玩儿。"汤姆回答。

"能让我刷刷这篱笆吗?"本问。

"这个嘛,好吧,但你得给我点儿东西。"汤姆回答。

"我只有这只死猫。"本回答。

汤姆接过死猫,给了本一把刷子。

名人名言

Nothing in the world is difficult for one who sets his mind to it.

世上无难事，只怕有心人。

paintbrush.

A little while later, some boys came along. They saw Ben having lots of fun painting the fence.

"Can I paint the fence? I'll give you this apple," said one boy.

"Okay," agreed Tom.

Soon, the other boys wanted to paint the fence.

paintbrush *n.* 油漆刷

agree *v.* 同意

过了一小会儿，几个男孩经过这里。他们看见本正刷篱笆刷得很开心。

"能让我刷刷这篱笆吗？我给你这个苹果。"一个男孩说。

"好吧。"汤姆同意了。

很快，其他的男孩都想来刷篱笆。

"I can give you a glass of lemonade," said one boy.

lemonade *n.* 柠檬

"And I can give you an old knife," said another. Tom smiled and sat under a tree, eating his apple and drinking his lemonade.

smile *v.* 笑

Aunt Polly was very surprised when she saw the painted fence.

surprised *adj.* 惊讶的

"My Tom, you can work when you want

"我可以给你一杯柠檬水。"一个男孩说。

"我可以给你一把旧刀子。"另一个说。汤姆笑嘻嘻地坐到树下，吃着苹果、喝着柠檬水。

波莉姨妈看到刷好漆的篱笆惊讶极了。

"我的汤姆，只要你想干好，就能把活儿干得很好，是吧？"

to, can't you?" Tom smiled, but didn't tell her the truth.

truth *n.* 真相

Tom went out to play in the street.

Just then he saw a new girl.

She had beautiful blue eyes and long yellow hair.

beautiful *adj.* 美丽的

"Oh, what a beautiful girl! I think I am in love with her," Tom said to himself.

He stood on his hands and then did a

stand *v.* 站立

汤姆笑了，但是没告诉她实情。

汤姆到街上去玩儿。

就在这时，他看到一个新来的女孩。

她有一双漂亮的蓝眼睛和一头金色长发。

"哦，多漂亮的女孩！我想我爱上她了。"汤姆心里想。

他倒立起来，又做了个侧翻，想炫耀一下。

cartwheel to show off.

But the girl just went into her house.

When Tom went back home, he learned about the new girl.

Her name was Becky and she had just moved into Tom's village.

For the rest of the day Tom could only think of Becky.

Tom hated Mondays.

cartwheel *n.* 侧手翻

village *n.* 村庄

hate *v.* 讨厌

但是女孩径直回了家。

汤姆回家以后，知道了这新来的女孩是谁。

她叫贝姬，刚刚搬到汤姆的村子。

那天剩下的时间里，汤姆满脑子想的都是贝姬。

汤姆讨厌星期一。

Mondays meant the beginning of a whole week of school.

On the way to school Tom saw Huckleberry Finn.

"Hello, Tom! Are you going to school? How unfortunate!" said Huck.

Huck never went to school.

He never washed his face or brushed his hair.

beginning *n.* 开始

unfortunate *adj.* 不幸的

never *adv.* 从不

星期一意味着要开始整整一个星期都去上学。

在去学校的路上，汤姆遇到了哈克贝利·费恩。

"你好，汤姆！你要去上学吗？真不幸！"哈克说。

哈克从来不上学。

他也从不洗脸梳头。

名人名言

Nothing is difficult to the man who will try.

世上无难事，只要肯登攀。

All the kids in the village were very jealous of him.

jealous *adj.* 嫉妒的

"Tom, shall we go to the graveyard tonight? Only brave boys can go there at midnight," said Huck.

graveyard *n.* 墓地

midnight *n.* 半夜

"Of course I will go with you," answered Tom.

"Okay, see you tonight!" said Huck.

tonight *n.* 今晚

村子里的孩子们都非常嫉妒他。

"汤姆，今天夜里我们去墓地怎么样？只有勇敢的男孩才能半夜去那儿。"哈克说。

"我当然跟你一起去。"汤姆回答。

"好吧，今晚见！"哈克说。

MCGRAW-HILL

The Big Promise

Tom and Huck walked through the tall grass of the graveyard.

The wind blowing through the trees sounded like ghosts.

blow *v.* 吹

ghost *n.* 鬼

Tom and Huck became scared.

scared *adj.* 害怕的

"Look! There!" said Tom in surprise.

surprise *n.* 惊讶

"What? What is it, Tom?" cried Huck.

"I saw something coming from over there," said Tom.

重要的许诺

汤姆和哈克走过墓地高高的草丛。

风吹过树林的声音听起来好像鬼魂在叫。

汤姆和哈克害怕了。

"看！那里！"汤姆惊讶地说。

"什么？那是什么，汤姆？"哈克叫道。

"我看见有东西正从那边过来。"汤姆说。

Both boys looked at the scary looking trees.

Slowly, through the darkness, three people appeared.

darkness *n.* 黑暗

appear *v.* 出现

It was Muff Potter, Injun Joe and Dr. Robinson. The three men were talking. Soon, they started fighting.

fight *v.* 打架

The doctor hit Potter on the head with a wooden board.

wooden *adj.* 木头的

两个男孩看着模样狰狞的树丛。

慢慢地，三个人影从黑暗中显现出来。

他们是穆夫·波特、印江·乔和罗宾逊医生。那三个人正在交谈。很快，他们开始打起架来。

医生用一块木板打中了波特的头。

It knocked Potter out.

Just then, Injun Joe picked up Potter's knife and stabbed Dr. Robinson.

When Potter woke up, he saw the doctor lying dead on the ground.

Potter's knife was sticking out of the doctor's back.

"What did I do?" cried Potter.

"You killed the doctor," Injun Joe lied

knock *v.* 敲

stab *v.* 捅

kill *v.* 杀死

波特被打晕了。

就在这时，印江·乔捡起波特的刀，捅了罗宾逊医生。

波特醒来的时候，看到医生倒在地上，已经死了。

波特的刀还插在医生的背上。

“我干了什么？”波特叫起来。

“你杀了医生。”印江·乔对波特说了谎。

to Potter.

Potter began crying and shaking.

shake *v.* 发抖

The boys were very frightened and ran all the way home.

frightened *adj.* 害怕的

"We have to tell someone," said Tom.

"But then Injun Joe will kill us. We must promise not to tell anyone," said Huck.

promise *v.* 保证

Tom agreed and they made a promise.

After Huck left, Tom went to bed.

波特哭了起来，怕得发抖。

两个男孩吓坏了，一溜烟跑回了家。

"我们得把这事告诉别人。"汤姆说。

"可那样的话，印第·乔会杀了我们。我们必须互相保证决不告诉任何人。"哈克说。汤姆同意了，他们彼此许诺。

哈克走后，汤姆上床睡觉。

名人名言

Nothing seek, nothing find.

没有追求就没有收获。

But he did not sleep well.

Dr. Robinson's body was found at noon the next day.

body *n.* 尸体

Somebody found Potter's knife in Dr. Robinson's back. Injun Joe told everyone Potter killed the doctor. Potter was put in the jail.

jail *n.* 监狱

Tom and Huck felt very guilty about what happened to Potter.

guilty *adj.* 内疚的

可是他睡得很不踏实。

罗宾逊医生的尸体第二天中午被发现了。

有人在罗宾逊医生的背上发现了波特的刀。印孔·乔对所有人说是波特杀了医生。波特被关进了监狱。

汤姆和哈克为波特的遭遇感到很内疚。

THE ADVENTURES OF TOM SAWYER

Walking through the village, they met their friend, Joe Harper.

He was also very sad. "What's wrong?" asked Tom.

"My mom punished me for eating some ice cream. But I swear I didn't eat it," said Joe.

punish v. 惩罚

swear v. 发誓

All three boys felt no one loved them.

They decided to run away.

decide v. 决定

他们在村子里闲逛的时候遇到了他们的朋友乔·哈珀。

他也很不开心。"出了什么事?"汤姆问。

"我妈妈罚我，她觉得我偷吃了冰激凌。可是我发誓我没吃。"乔说。

三个男孩都觉得没有人爱他们。

他们决定出走。

"Where shall we go?" asked Joe.

"We can go down the river to an island," said Tom.

island *n.* 岛

"We will become pirates!" cried Huck.

"Okay, let's meet at the river tonight," said Tom.

Tom, Huck and Joe pushed off in a raft that night.

raft *n.* 竹筏

It moved down the river slowly.

"我们去哪儿呢?" 乔问。

"我们可以沿河顺流而下,去一个岛上。" 汤姆说。

"我们可以当海盗!" 哈克大叫。

"好吧,今晚我们就在河边碰面。" 汤姆说。

那天晚上,汤姆、哈克和乔乘着木筏离开了岸边。

木筏缓缓地顺流而下。

A while later, they reached an island.

Lying under the stars, they fell asleep.

The next morning the three boys caught some fish and ate them for breakfast.

In the afternoon they saw some boats on the river.

They also heard people shouting.

"They are probably looking for us,"

reach *v.* 到达

shout *v.* 叫喊

probably *adv.* 可能

不一会儿，他们就到了一个小岛。

他们躺在星空下睡着了。

第二天早上，三个男孩钓了些鱼，当早饭吃了。

下午，他们看到河上有几条船。

他们也听到了人们在叫喊。

"他们可能正在找我们。"汤姆说。

said Tom.

"But we can never go back home," said Joe.

The boys continued to fish, but soon they became bored.

That night they felt homesick and lonely.

The next day, Joe and Huck wanted to go home.

continue *v.* 继续

bored *adj.* 厌倦的

homesick *adj.* 想家的

"但我们不能回家。"乔说。

男孩们继续钓鱼，可是很快他们就觉得没意思了。

那天晚上，他们都开始想家，感觉孤独极了。

第二天，乔和哈克想回家了。

名人名言

Nothing is so necessary for travelers as languages.

外出旅行，语言最重要。

"Listen, I have a great idea!"

Tom told them his wonderful plan.

Joe and Huck loved the plan.

They agreed to stay another night.　　another *adj.* 另一个

On Sunday morning the bells rang slowly in the village.

It was the day of the three boys' funeral.　　funeral *n.* 葬礼

Many people were crying in the church.　　church *n.* 教堂

"听着，我有个好主意！"

汤姆把自己绝妙的计划说给他们听。

乔和哈克都很喜欢这个计划。

他们同意再待一夜。

星期天早上，村子里响起低缓的丧钟。

这天是为三个男孩举行葬礼的日子。

教堂里很多人都在哭泣。

Suddenly the door opened.

The boys walked into the church.

That was Tom's big plan.

"Oh, my Tom! I am so happy to see you again," cried Aunt Polly.

"Tom, I am happy to see you, too," said Becky.

It was the best day of his life.

suddenly *adv.* 突然地

plan *n.* 计划

突然，门开了。

男孩们走进了教堂。

这就是汤姆的重大计划。

"哦，我的汤姆！我真高兴能再见到你。"波莉姨妈哭着说。

"汤姆，我也很高兴见到你。"贝姬说。

这是汤姆有生以来最棒的一天。

A Brave Boy Tom Sawyer

The next few months of school went by slowly.

Tom was still very worried about Muff Potter.

worried *adj.* 担心的

"Huck, I want to help Potter," said Tom.

"I do, too. But I am afraid of Injun Joe," said Huck sadly.

afraid *adj.* 害怕的

At last, the day of the trial came, and everyone in the village sat in the

trial *n.* 审判

勇敢的汤姆·索亚

之后几个月在每天上学放学中慢慢过去。

汤姆仍然很担心穆夫·波特。

"哈克，我想帮助波特。"汤姆说。

"我也想。可是我害怕印泜·乔。"哈克难过地说。

最后，审判的日子到了，村子里的人都坐在法庭上旁听。

courtroom.

Injun Joe appeared and repeated his lie.

Everyone believed Potter had killed Dr. Robinson.

Suddenly Potter's lawyer shouted, "Here is a witness! Tom Sawyer, come up here." Everyone looked at Tom in surprise.

"Tom, where were you on that night?"

courtroom *n.* 法庭

lawyer *n.* 律师

witness *n.* 目击者；
证人

印江·乔出来重复了一遍他的谎言。

大家都相信是波特杀了罗宾逊医生。

突然，波特的律师大喊道："这里有一位目击者！汤姆·索亚，到这里来。"所有人都惊讶地看着汤姆。

"汤姆，那天晚上你在哪里？"波特的律师问。

asked Potter's lawyer.

"I was in the graveyard," answered Tom.

Tom looked afraid, but he didn't stop talking.

"I saw everything. It was Injun Joe, not Potter. Injun Joe killed the doctor."

Everyone gasped.

everything *pron.* 一切

gasp *v.* 倒抽气

"我在墓地。"汤姆回答。

汤姆看上去很害怕，但还是继续说了下去。

"我看到了一切。杀人的是印泓·乔，不是波特。是印泓·乔杀了医生。"

大家都倒吸了一口凉气。

名人名言

Nothing is to be got without pains but poverty.

世上唯有贫穷可以不劳而获。

Crash!

Injun Joe had broken a window and leapt through it.

The police looked for Injun Joe but could not find him.

Tom and Huck had bad dreams that night.

However, one thing helped Tom and Huck feel better.

break *v.* （使）破

leap *v.* 跳

however *adv.* 然而

砰！

印汜·乔打破了窗子，跳了出去。

警察到处搜捕印汜·乔，但是没能找到他。

那天晚上，汤姆和哈克都做了噩梦。

不过，有一件事让汤姆和哈克感觉好了一些。

It was looking for treasure. Tom had read that robbers usually hid their treasure in haunted houses.

One day, Tom and Huck decided to explore the haunted house near their village.

They tiptoed quietly into the house.

The inside of the house was dark and dusty.

treasure *n.*
金银财宝

haunted *adj.* 闹鬼的

explore *v.* 探索；勘查

tiptoe *v.* 踮着脚走

那就是寻宝。汤姆从书上看到强盗们通常都会把他们的财宝藏在闹鬼的房子里。

一天，汤姆和哈克决定去村子附近的一个鬼屋探险。

他们悄悄地溜进那座房子。

房子里很暗，到处都是灰尘。

Suddenly they heard footsteps coming from outside.

They were very surprised and hid upstairs.

They found a hole and looked down through the floor.

"Oh, no!" said Tom.

"Who is it?" asked Huck.

"It's Injun Joe and another man,"

footstep *n.* 脚步声

hide *v.* 躲藏

upstairs *adv.* 在楼上

突然，他们听到外面有脚步声传来。

他们非常惊讶，藏到了楼上。

他们在地板上发现了一个洞，于是透过洞看下去。

"哦，不！"汤姆说。

"是谁？"哈克问。

"是印没·乔和另一个人。"汤姆屏着气说。

THE ADVENTURES OF TOM SAWYER

gasped Tom.

"Where are we going to hide this bag of silver coins?" asked the man.

silver *n.* 银

"Here, under the fireplace," answered Injun Joe.

fireplace *n.* 壁炉

He began digging under the fireplace.

dig *v.* 挖

"Oh, something is here!" shouted Injun Joe.

"What is it, what have you found?"

"我们把这袋银币藏到哪里呢?"男人问。

"这里，在壁炉下面。"印弟·乔回答。

他开始在壁炉下面挖起来。

"哦，这里有东西!"印弟·乔叫道。

"是什么?你发现了什么?"男人问。

asked the man.

"Look at this! It's full of gold coins," exclaimed Injun Joe.

exclaim *v.* 惊叫

"Whose is it?" asked the man.

"The old Carter Gang used to hang out here. They must have buried it before they were caught by the police," said Injun Joe.

hang out 常去某处

bury *v.* 埋

"What shall we do?" asked the man.

~~~~~~~~~~~~~~~~~~~~~~~~~~~~~~~~~~

"看看这个！里面全都是金币。"印弟·乔惊叫起来。

"这是谁的呢？"男人问。

"老卡特那伙人过去经常在这附近出没。他们在被警察抓走前，肯定是把钱埋在这儿了。"印弟·乔说。

"我们怎么办？"男人问。

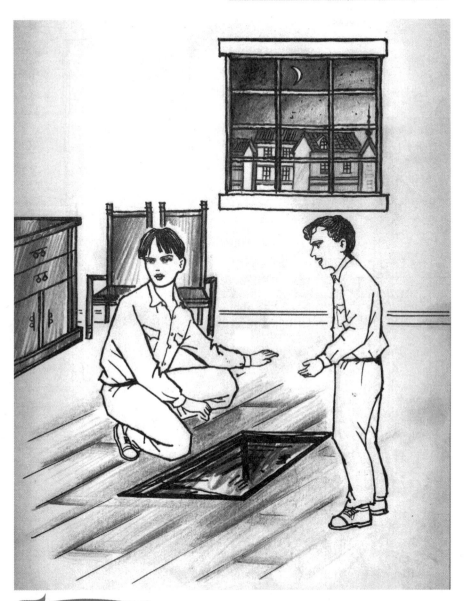

名人名言

Not to advance is to go back.

不进则退。

"Let's bury it with our bag of silver coins," answered Injun Joe.

Just then, Injun Joe heard a noise from upstairs and looked up.

noise *n.* 响声

"Someone must be upstairs," said Injun Joe.

The two boys turned white with fear.

Injun Joe started to go upstairs, but the steps collapsed under his weight.

collapse *v.* 倒塌

"我们把这些跟我们的银币埋在一起吧。"印弟·乔回答。

就在这时，印弟·乔听到楼上有动静，抬头看了上去。

"楼上肯定有人。"印弟·乔说。

两个男孩吓得脸都白了。

印弟·乔抬脚上楼，但是一下子把楼梯踩断了。

"Come on, Joe. There is no one here except us!" shouted the man.

except *prep.*
除······之外

"You're right. But I should take the treasure to a different hiding place," said Injun Joe. "Where?" asked the man.

"Underneath a white cross. Let's get out of here," said Injun Joe.

underneath *prep.*
在······下面

Injun Joe and the man disappeared with the bags of treasure.

disappear *v.* 消失

"好了，乔。这里除了我们没有别人！"男人喊道。

"你说得对。不过我要把财宝换到别的地方藏起来。"印泓·乔说。"什么地方？"男人问。

"在白色十字下面。我们出去吧。"印泓·乔说。

印泓·乔和男人带着装有财宝的袋子消失了。

But where was the white cross?

The Hidden Treasure

"Wow, today's the school picnic!" exclaimed Tom.

picnic *n.* 野餐

Tom was happy because he was going with Becky.

The picnic was held next to a huge cave.

hold *v.* 举办

After eating and playing, someone

someone *pron.* 某人

可是那个白色十字究竟在哪儿呢?

隐藏的财宝

"哇,今天是学校野餐的日子!"汤姆惊叫道。

汤姆很开心,因为他要跟贝姬一块儿去。

野餐地点就在一个巨大的山洞旁边。

吃喝玩闹一通之后,有人说:"我们为什么不去山洞探险?"

said, "Why don't we explore the cave?"

Everyone took candles and walked into the cave. The cave was large, mysterious and romantic.

candle *n.* 蜡烛	
mysterious *adj.* 神秘的	

The children played in the cave. They hid in the darkness, trying to scare one another.

Tom and Becky ventured further and further into the cave.

venture *v.* 冒险去（某处）

于是大家拿上蜡烛，走进了山洞。山洞非常大，充满了神秘和浪漫的色彩。

孩子们在山洞里打闹。他们藏在暗处，想吓别人一跳。

汤姆和贝姬在洞里越走越深。

"Look at those bats!" shouted Tom.

Tom and Becky chased them into the passage.

"Tom, let's go back now," said Becky.

"Oh, Becky! I can't find the way out," said Tom.

"We are lost!" cried Becky.

They walked and walked until they were very tired.

bat	*n.*	蝙蝠
chase	*v.*	追
passage	*n.*	通道
go back		回去

"看那些蝙蝠!"汤姆喊道。

汤姆和贝姬追着蝙蝠跑进了岔道。

"汤姆,现在我们回去吧。"贝姬说。

"哦,贝姬!我找不到出去的路了。"汤姆说。

"我们迷路了!"贝姬哭了起来。

他们走啊走啊,一直走到筋疲力尽。

名人名言

Not to know what happened before one was born is always to be a child.

不懂世故，幼稚可笑。

Slowly their last candle went out. It was completely dark in the cave. They slept for a while, but they woke up because of some noise. Tom crawled down a passage and then he gasped. It was Injun Joe! Fortunately Injun Joe didn't see Tom and just went away.

Three days passed.

Everyone believed Tom and Becky

completely *adv.*
完全地

crawl *v.* 爬

他们的最后一根蜡烛也慢慢熄灭了。洞里一片漆黑。他们睡了一会儿，但是被什么动静惊醒了。汤姆顺着一条岔道往前爬，接着倒吸了一口凉气。那是印丕·乔！幸运的是，印丕·乔没有看到汤姆，径自走了。

三天过去了。

所有人都相信汤姆和贝姬已经死了。半夜里，教堂的钟声突然

were dead. In the middle of the night, the church bells suddenly began ringing.

People shouted, "They're found, they're found!" It was the greatest night the village had ever had. Tom and Becky told everyone about their adventure.

"I found a hole in the wall. Then I returned to the cave and carried Becky out," said Tom confidently.

adventure n. 冒险经历

return v. 回去；返回

confidently adv. 自信地

响了起来。

　　人们喊着："找到他们了，找到他们了！"这是村子有史以来最棒的一夜。汤姆和贝姬给大家讲了他们的冒险经历。

　　"我在山壁上找到了一个出口。然后我回到洞里把贝姬背了出来。"汤姆自信地说。

"A fisherman saw us and took us back to the village," said Becky.

fisherman *n.* 渔夫

Tom was a hero again.

hero *n.* 英雄

A week later, Tom went to see Becky at her house.

"Would you ever go back into the cave?" asked Becky's father.

"Maybe," said Tom slowly.

slowly *adv.* 慢慢地

"That is why I put a big door on the

"一个渔夫看到了我们，把我们送回了村子。"贝姬说。

汤姆又成了英雄。

一个星期以后，汤姆去贝姬家看望她。

"你还会再去那个山洞里吗？"贝姬的父亲问。

"也许吧。"汤姆慢吞吞地说。

"所以我给那山洞装了个大门还上了锁。"

cave and locked it."

Tom turned completely white.

"But Injun Joe may be inside!" he cried.

The police ran to the cave and opened the door.

They found Injun Joe inside the cave.

He had starved to death.

Tom and Huck felt sad, but now they

inside *adv.* 在里面

police *n.* 警察

starve *v.* 挨饿

汤姆顿时脸变白了。

"可是印江·乔可能在里面！"他叫道。

警察跑到山洞，打开了门。

他们发现印江·乔在洞里。

他已经饿死了。

汤姆和哈克感到很难过，不过现在他们安全了。

were safe.

The next day, Tom asked Huck, "Will you go to the cave with me? I think the treasure is there."

Huck jumped up and said, "Let's go to the cave!"

Tom led Huck to the spot in the cave.

"Look at this! It is a white cross," shouted Huck.

safe *adj.* 安全的

jump *v.* 跳

spot *n.* 地点

第二天，汤姆问哈克："你愿意跟我到洞里去吗？我想财宝就在那里。"

哈克跳了起来，说："我们走吧！"

汤姆领着哈克到了洞里的那个地方。

"看这个！是白色十字。"哈克喊道。

名人名言

No way is impossible to courage.

勇者无惧。

They dug and dug and finally found two bags of gold and silver coins.

"We are rich!" exclaimed Tom and Huck.

They ran back to the village and showed the treasure to the people.

Tom and Huck continued to be best friends.

And they continued to have lots of adventures together.

finally *adv.* 最终

continue *v.* 继续

together *adv.* 一起

他们挖呀挖，终于找到了装着金币和银币的两个袋子。

"我们有钱了！"汤姆和哈克欢呼起来。

他们跑回村子，把财宝给人们看。

汤姆和哈克仍然是最好的朋友。

他们在一起又经历了许多冒险。

MCGRAW-HILL

Don Quixote

堂·吉诃德

Don Quixote of La Mancha

Alonso Quixano was a middle-aged gentleman in La Mancha.

He lived with his young niece.

He liked to read stories about knights.

He spent most of his time reading.

One day Alonso said to his niece and his friends, the curate and the barber, "I've decided to become a knight. From

gentleman *n.* 绅士

knight *n.* 骑士

curate *n.* 牧师

拉曼查的堂·吉诃德

阿隆索·吉哈诺是位中年绅士，住在拉曼查。

他和他年轻的外甥女一起生活。

他喜欢看有关骑士的故事。

他把大部分时间都用来看书。

一天，阿隆索对他的外甥女和朋友们——牧师和剃头匠——

now on my name is Don Quixote and my horse will be called Rosinante."

"A knight without a lady is like a tree without fruit. Dulcinea del Toboso will be the lady of my heart," Don Quixote said to himself.

In fact, Dulcinea was just a country girl. Her real name was Aldonza Lorenzo and Don Quixote had never seen her

without *prep.* 没有

country *n.* 乡下

real *adj.* 真正的

说："我决心要成为骑士。从现在起，我就叫堂·吉诃德了，我的马叫罗西南多。"

"一个骑士没有美人相伴就好像一棵树结不出果实。托博索的杜尔西内亚就是我的心上人。" 堂·吉诃德对自己如是说。

实际上，杜尔西内亚不过是个乡下姑娘。

她真名叫阿尔冬萨·洛伦索。堂·吉诃德以前从来没有见过

before.

Soon Don Quixote began to prepare
to be a knight. He polished his great-
grandfather's armor and helmet.

"All right, I'm ready to travel the world!"
Don Quixote exclaimed and left his home
village.

Now Don Quixote had a big problem.

A knight needed to be dubbed by a

prepare *v.* 准备

polish *v.* 擦亮

armor *n.* 盔甲

dub *v.* 给……起绰号

她。

很快，堂•吉诃德就开始着手准备把自己变成骑士。他把曾祖父的盔甲和头盔擦得闪闪发亮。

"好了，我可以去周游世界了！"堂•吉诃德大叫起来。然后，他离开了村子。

这时，堂•吉诃德遇到了一个大麻烦。

因为骑士需要得到住在城堡里的贵族的册封。

lord in a castle.

Soon he arrived at an inn, but he thought it was a castle.

"What a nice castle! I'll stay here tonight," he said.

Then he knelt before the innkeeper and said, "My Lord, I wish to be dubbed."

The innkeeper was surprised at first.

But he decided to make fun of this

castle *n.* 城堡

inn *n.* 客栈

innkeeper *n.*
客栈老板

没过多久，他来到一家客栈，不过他把它想象成了一座城堡。

"真是座宏伟的城堡！我要在这里过夜。"他说。

然后他跪在了客栈老板面前说："大人，我希望获得您的册封。"

客栈老板一开始吃了一惊。

不过他决定捉弄一下这个神经病。

mad man.

With a sword he hit Don Quixote on the shoulder and said, "I dub you a knight."

sword *n.* 剑

"Ouch!" Don Quixote felt pain, but he was very happy.

pain *n.* 疼痛

The newly-dubbed knight left the inn for adventure.

He met a group of merchants on the road.

merchant *n.* 商人

他拿了把剑在堂·吉诃德肩头一拍，说："我封你为骑士啦。"

"哎哟！"堂·吉诃德觉得肩膀被拍得生疼，但他心里却很高兴。

这位新受封的骑士离开客栈，踏上冒险的旅程。

途中他遇到了一队商人。

 名人名言

Obedience is the first duty of a soldier.

军人以服从命令为天职。

Don Quixote said to them, "No one can go from here. You must first say that Dulcinea del Toboso is the most beautiful lady."

The merchants said, "What is this man talking about?"

talk about 谈论

Don Quixote became angry and tried to attack them. But Rosinante stumbled and Don Quixote fell to the ground.

stumble *v.* 绊脚；
绊倒

堂·吉诃德对他们说："你们得先说'托博索的杜尔西内亚是天下第一美人'，否则谁都别想从这儿过。"

商人们说："这个家伙在胡说些什么？"

堂·吉诃德火冒三丈，准备去攻击这些商人。可是罗西南多马失前蹄，堂·吉诃德摔了个嘴啃泥。

The merchants laughed and beat him.

After they left, a farmer from La Mancha came by and saw the poor knight.

"What's the matter, Don Quixote?" he asked.

"I fought ten giants and fell off my horse," Don Quixote answered.

The farmer took Don Quixote to his

beat *v.* 打

come by 经过

giant *n.* 巨人

商人们大笑起来，把堂・吉诃德暴打一顿。

他们走后，一个拉曼查来的农夫从这里经过，看到了可怜的骑士。

"出了什么事儿，堂・吉诃德?"他问。

"我跟十个巨人作战时从马上摔下来了。"堂・吉诃德答道。

农夫把堂・吉诃德送回了家。

home.

When Don Quixote got better, he wanted to continue his adventure. He met a farmer named Sancho Panza.

"I'm Don Quixote of La Mancha. You will be my servant from now on. We will fight evil for Lady Dulcinea," said Don Quixote.

Sancho was just a poor farmer.

servant *n.* 仆人

evil *n.* 邪恶

poor *adj.* 可怜的

堂·吉诃德恢复一点儿以后，又想继续去冒险。他遇到了一个叫桑丘·潘沙的农夫。

"我是拉曼查的堂·吉诃德。从现在起，你就是我的仆人了。我们要去与邪恶势力作战，保护杜尔西内亚小姐。"堂·吉诃德说。

桑丘不过是个穷得叮当响的农夫。

He was not interested in knights or their adventures.

He only wanted some money.

"How will you pay me?" asked Sancho.

"We will have an island. I will make you the governor of it," said Don Quixote.

"Very good! I will be your servant," said Sancho.

interested *adj.* 感兴趣的	
pay *v.* 付费；付酬	
governor *n.* 总督	

他对骑士或是冒险什么的一点儿兴趣也没有。

他只想挣点儿钱。

"您打算怎么付我钱呢？"桑丘问。

"我们会拥有一个岛，我就让你当这个岛的总督吧。"堂·吉诃德说。

"太好了！我愿意当您的仆人。"桑丘说。

The Brave Knight

In the morning, Don Quixote and Sancho were in a field.

There were thirty or forty windmills.

windmill *n.* 风车

"Can you see the giants, Sancho?" cried Don Quixote.

"What giants? They're windmills!" said Sancho.

But Don Quixote was already riding toward the windmills.

already *adv.* 已经

toward *prep.* 向

勇敢的骑士

早上，堂·吉诃德和桑丘来到一片田野。

这里有三四十座风车。

"看到那些巨人了吗，桑丘？"堂·吉诃德叫道。

"什么巨人？那是风车啊！"桑丘说。

可是堂·吉诃德已经策马冲向了风车。

名人名言

Observation is the best teacher.

观察是最好的老师。

As soon as he rode into the windmill, he and his horse were thrown back.

throw back 掷回

"I told you they were windmills!" cried Sancho.

"A witch changed the giants into windmills," said the poor knight.

change *v.* 改变

One rainy day, Don Quixote and Sancho were walking in the forest. From far away Don Quixote saw another

rainy *adj.* 下雨的

他和马儿刚冲向风车的扇叶就被甩了回来。

"我告诉过您那些是风车!"桑丘叫起来。

"有个巫婆把这些巨人变成了风车。"可怜的骑士说。

一个下雨天,堂·吉诃德和桑丘在森林里赶路。堂·吉诃德看到远处有位骑士。

knight.

"That knight is wearing a golden helmet," he said.

golden *adj.* 金的

"He's not a knight and it's not a helmet. I think he is a barber with a basin on his head," said Sancho.

barber *n.* 理发师

"No! He is a knight with a golden helmet. I will fight him off," said Don Quixote.

fight off 打败

"那位骑士戴着金头盔呢。"他说。

"他根本就不是骑士，戴的也不是头盔，我看那是个剃头的，脑袋上顶着个盆。"桑丘说。

"不对！他就是位戴着金头盔的骑士，我要打败他。" 堂·吉诃德说。

He ran with his lance but Sancho was right.

The man was a traveling barber. When the barber saw Don Quixote, he was scared and ran away.

"Hooray! I beat the enemy!" exclaimed Don Quixote.

Don Quixote and Sancho rode up a mountain.

lance *n.* 长矛

run away 逃跑

hooray *n.* 万岁

他握着长矛冲上去，可桑丘说得没错。

这是个走街串巷的剃头匠。剃头的看到堂·吉诃德后被吓坏了，落荒而逃。

"万岁！我打败了敌人！"堂·吉诃德欢呼起来。

堂·吉诃德和桑丘驱马上了一座山。

"You must give my letter to Lady Dulcinea. I will stay and wait here," said Don Quixote. When Sancho saw the letter, he was surprised.

"Is your lady the daughter of Lorenzo Corchuleo? Well, she's my neighbor!"

neighbor *n.* 邻居

"Her background doesn't matter. Lady Dulcinea is the greatest princess in the world," said Don Quixote.

background *n.* 背景

princess *n.* 公主

"你得把我写给杜尔西内亚小姐的信给她送去。我就待在这儿等着。"堂·吉诃德说。桑丘看到信以后吃了一惊。

"您的爱人就是洛伦索·考述里奥的女儿吗？呃，她是我的邻居呢！"

"她的出身并不重要。杜尔西内亚小姐是世界上最美的公主。"堂·吉诃德说。

Sancho left for Toboso.

On the way he met Don Quixote's friends, the curate and the barber.

"How's your master?" asked the curate.

"He's on the mountain," answered Sancho.

"We have to go and save him," said the barber.

leave for 出发去某地

master *n.* 主人

桑丘动身前往托博索。

途中他遇到了堂·吉诃德的朋友——牧师和剃头匠。

"你的主人怎么样了?"牧师问。

"在山上呢。"桑丘回答。

"我们得去救他。"剃头匠说。

名人名言

Offense is the best defense.

进攻是最好的防御。

They asked a girl to help them.

The girl, the curate, the barber and Sancho went up the mountain. The girl dressed up as a princess.

dress up 打扮

Then she went to Don Quixote and said, "I'm Princess Micomicona. A giant killed my father and took his crown. Please help me, brave knight!"

crown *n.* 王冠

brave *adj.* 勇敢的

他们请一位姑娘帮忙。

那位姑娘、牧师、剃头匠和桑丘上了山。姑娘打扮成公主的样子。

然后她走到堂·吉诃德面前，说："我是米可米可娜公主。一个巨人杀了我的父亲，夺走了他的王冠。请救救我，勇敢的骑士！"

"Don't worry. I will kill the wicked giant, Princess," said Don Quixote.

wicked *adj.* 邪恶的

The girl led Don Quixote to his home village.

On the way they met Don Quixote's friends and Sancho.

on the way 在途中

That night, they arrived at an inn.

arrive at 到达

Don Quixote and Sancho slept in one of the rooms.

"别担心，公主，我会杀死那邪恶的巨人的。" 堂·吉诃德说。

姑娘带着堂·吉诃德向他住的村庄走去。

路上他们遇到了堂·吉诃德的朋友们和桑丘。

当夜，他们在一家客栈投宿。

堂·吉诃德和桑丘到一间屋里去睡觉了。

The others were eating in the dining room.

Suddenly Sancho rushed in and cried, "Help! Help! My master is fighting with the giant!"

Everyone ran to Don Quixote's room.

He was swinging his sword, wearing only a shirt and a helmet.

"I cut the giant into pieces! Princess

rush *v.* 冲

fight with 与……争斗

piece *n.* 块；片；段

其他人则在餐厅里吃东西。

突然，桑丘冲进来大喊："救命！救命！主人在跟巨人搏斗！"

大家都冲向堂·吉诃德的房间。

他只穿了件衬衫，戴着头盔，手舞足蹈地挥着剑。

"我把巨人砍得稀巴烂了！米可米可娜公主可以收复她的王国

Micomicona will get her kingdom back!"
Don Quixote shouted.

kingdom *n.* 王国

In his sleep, he had thought the wineskins were part of the giant. The wine from the wineskins had split everywhere.

wineskin *n.* 酒囊

split *v.* 分裂

"Oh, my wineskins!" cried the innkeeper.

"I defeated the evil giant!" cried Don

defeat *v.* 打败

了!"堂•吉诃德大喊着。

在睡梦中，他误将葡萄酒袋看成巨人了。酒袋里的酒溅得到处都是。

"嗷，我的酒袋啊!"客栈老板尖叫起来。

"我打败了邪恶的巨人!"堂•吉诃德大喊大叫着。

Quixote.

The curate said to the innkeeper, "Don't worry. I'll pay for the wineskins and wine."

pay for 为……付钱

The fight with the wineskins had made Don Quixote very tired.

tired *adj.* 疲惫的

He fell asleep again.

The barber and the curate put him in a cage. Then they put the cage on a cart.

cart *n.* 马车

牧师对客栈老板说："别担心，我会赔偿酒袋和酒的钱。"

和酒袋搏斗的堂·吉诃德筋疲力尽。

他又进入了梦乡。

剃头匠和牧师把他关进笼子里，然后把笼子装上马车。马车向着他们住的村庄驶去。

名人名言

Old friends and old wines are best.

陈酒味醇，老友情深。

The cart headed for their home village.

When Don Quixote woke up, he was very surprised.

"Where am I now? Why am I in a cage?" he yelled.

The barber said, "You're flying in a sky cart. You will meet your love Lady Dulcinea."

head *v.* 朝着……行进

wake up 醒来

yell *v.* 叫喊

堂·吉诃德醒来后大吃一惊。

"我这是在哪儿?为什么被关在笼子里?"他叫起来。

剃头匠说:"你正坐着一辆会飞的马车飞呢。你很快就能见到你心爱的杜尔西内亚小姐了。"

More Adventures

Don Quixote and his friends arrived at their home village.

Sancho's wife was happy to see her husband.

"Have you bought a pretty dress for me?" asked his wife.

pretty *adj.* 漂亮的

"I'm sorry, but my master and I are going to get an island. I'll be the governor of the island," said Sancho.

更多的冒险

堂·吉诃德和朋友们回到了他们生活的村庄。

桑丘的老婆看到老公回来很是高兴。

"你有没有给我买条漂亮裙子回来啊?"他老婆问。

"真对不住你啊,不过主人和我会得到一个岛呢。岛的总督就是我哦。"桑丘说。

His wife thought for a moment and said, "Well, I don't want to be the wife of the governor. I just want to have enough clothes and food."

A few days later, Don Quixote and Sancho began to talk about their next adventure.

Don Quixote's niece heard that her uncle was preparing for another adventure.

moment	n. 瞬间；片刻
enough	adj. 足够的
a few	一些
niece	n. 外甥女

他老婆想了一会儿，然后说："唉，我可不想当什么总督夫人。我就想着衣食无忧就可以了。"

几天后，堂·吉诃德和桑丘开始讨论下一次冒险之旅。

堂·吉诃德的外甥女听说舅舅又要去冒险。

She came to him and said, "Please stay home, Uncle. You are old, weak and poor. How could you be a strong and brave knight? Please look at yourself."

weak *adj.* 虚弱的

Don Quixote said kindly, "You don't understand. Never mind me and do your work."

kindly *adv.* 慈祥地

understand *v.*

明白；理解

Don Quixote and Sancho left their home village again.

她走到他面前说："请留在家里吧，舅舅。您年纪大了，身体又不好，还没什么钱。您怎么能成为强壮、勇敢的骑士呢？请好好看看您自己吧。"

堂·吉诃德慈祥地说："你不明白。别管我了，去干活儿吧。"

堂·吉诃德和桑丘又一次离开了村庄。

The next day they met another knight.

In fact, the new knight was Don Quixote's neighbor.

in fact 实际上

The village people had sent him to take Don Quixote back home.

The strange knight said, "I am the Knight of the Forest. I've beaten even the great Don Quixote of La Mancha. I made him say, 'Lady Casildea is the most

strange *adj.* 陌生的

forest *n.* 森林

第二天，他们遇到另一位骑士。

实际上，这位新骑士是堂·吉诃德的邻居。

是村民们派他来带堂·吉诃德回家的。

陌生的骑士说："我是森林骑士。我连伟大的拉曼查的堂·吉诃德都打败过。我还让他说出了'卡西尔迪亚小姐是天下第一美

 名人名言

Old sin makes new shame.

一失足成千古恨。

beautiful lady.'"

"What? I am Don Quixote of La Mancha. And no one can be more beautiful than Lady Dulcinea!" cried Don Quixote.

The two knights started to fight.

start *v.* 开始

But the Knight of the Forest lost the fight.

lose *v.* 输掉

Don Quixote felt very proud of himself.

女'这样的话。"

"什么?我就是拉曼查的堂·吉诃德。谁也比不上杜尔西内亚小姐漂亮!"堂·吉诃德叫道。

两位骑士开始战斗。

不过森林骑士一败涂地。

堂·吉诃德觉得非常骄傲。

One day Don Quixote saw a cart with flags.

flag *n.* 旗

"What do you have in your cart?" he asked.

"I have two lions. They're a present to the king from the general of Oran," the driver said.

lion *n.* 狮子

general *n.* 将军

"Oh, I must fight the beasts. I'm sure the witches have sent them. Open the

witch *n.* 女巫；巫婆

一天，堂·吉诃德看到一辆插着旗子的马车。

"车里装的什么?"他问。

"是两只狮子，是奥伦将军进献给国王的礼物。"车夫说。

"嗯，那我一定得跟这两只野兽斗一斗。我敢肯定是巫婆把它

cage right now, or I'll kill you," Don
Quixote said.

The driver opened the cage and hid
behind a tree. Don Quixote stood bravely
before the beasts. However, the lions
turned their back and sat down.

Quickly, the driver closed the cage door
and drove the cart away. Don Quixote
named himself "the Knight of the Lions."

right now 立刻

quickly *adv.* 很快地

们送来的。马上打开笼子，否则我就杀了你。"堂•吉诃德说。

车夫打开笼子，躲到一棵树后面。堂•吉诃德勇敢地站到狮子面前。可是，两只狮子转了个身，一屁股坐了下来。

车夫赶紧关上笼门，驱车而去。堂•吉诃德把自己命名为"猛

Sancho and Don Quixote arrived at an inn.

A puppeteer arrived with his puppets, also.

"Ladies and gentlemen, I'll begin the puppet show now. Please take your seat," the puppeteer said. Then he began his show.

puppeteer *n.*
演木偶剧的人

puppet *n.* 木偶

show *n.* 表演

狮骑士"。

桑丘和堂·吉诃德来到一家旅馆。

一个演木偶剧的艺人带着木偶也来到这里。

"女士们，先生们，现在我要开始演木偶剧了。请坐吧。"木偶戏艺人说。然后，他开始表演。

"This is the brave knight Don Gayferos and Lady Melisandra. The knight has just freed his lady from the evil Moors. Now the Moors are chasing the knight and his lady."

free *v.* 使摆脱；解放

Don Quixote suddenly stood up and shouted, "I must help that brave knight. None of you evil Moors will be saved!" He sliced all the Moorish puppets with his sword.

evil *adj.* 邪恶的

slice *v.* 将……切成片

"这是勇敢的骑士堂·盖费罗斯和梅丽桑德拉小姐。骑士刚刚把心上人从可怕的摩尔人那里解救出来。这时，摩尔人正在追赶骑士和他的爱人。"

堂·吉诃德突然站起来大喊："我得帮那位勇敢的骑士一把。你们这些可恶的摩尔人全都去死吧！"他用剑把所有摩尔人的木偶都砍成了碎片。

名人名言

Once a man and twice a child.

一次老，两次小。

The End of the Adventures

Sancho decided to ask for his payment.

"I think you should pay me now. You said you would give me an island," he said.

Don Quixote thought for a moment and replied, "Have you ever seen a knight's servant ask for his payment? Just like

ask for 要求……

payment *n.* 付款

reply *v.* 回答

~~~~~~~~~~~~~~~~~~~~~~~~~~~~~~

冒险的终结

桑丘决定讨要自己的薪水。

"我觉得您现在该付我钱了。您说过要给我一个岛的。"他说。

堂·吉诃德想了一下，回答道："你见过哪个骑士的仆人向他

you are doing with me now?"

Tears were forming up in Sancho's eyes.

"Please forgive me, Master. I'll never even think of my payment," he sobbed.

Don Quixote and Sancho continued their adventures.

One day they saw some hunters in the

tear *n.* 眼泪

forgive *v.* 原谅

sob *v.* 啜泣；呜咽

hunter *n.* 猎人

索要薪水的？就像你现在向我要钱一样？"

桑丘的眼中涌起了泪花。

"请原谅我，主人。我以后再也不去想什么薪水了。"他抽泣着说。

堂•吉诃德和桑丘继续冒险之旅。

一天，他们看到几位猎人在林中狩猎。

forest.

They were the Duke and Duchess.

"I'm the Knight of the Lions," Don Quixote said.

The Duke and Duchess decided to make fun of the knight and his servant.

"Oh, I've heard a lot about you. I'd like to invite you to our castle," said the Duchess.

make fun of 嘲弄

invite *v.* 邀请

是公爵和他的夫人。

"我是猛狮骑士。"堂·吉诃德说。

公爵和公爵夫人决定捉弄一下这位骑士和他的仆人。

"噢，真是久仰大名。我想请二位到我们的城堡做客。" 公爵夫人说。

"Thank you," Don Quixote said.

All the servants in the castle pretended to welcome Don Quixote and Sancho.

pretend *v.* 假装

But they laughed at the knight and his servant.

laugh *v.* 笑

The Duke and Duchess planned to play a trick on Don Quixote and Sancho.

One night, a girl with a veil over her face entered the castle. A man in black

veil *n.* 面纱

"谢谢。"堂·吉诃德说。

城堡里的所有佣人都假装欢迎堂·吉诃德和桑丘。

可背地里他们都嘲笑这位骑士和他的仆人。

公爵和公爵夫人决定戏弄一下堂·吉诃德和桑丘。

一天夜里，一个蒙着面纱的姑娘走进城堡。一个身着黑衣的男

stood beside her.

The man said to Sancho, "This is Lady Dulcinea. Lash yourself on your buttocks three thousand three hundred times. Then the spell on Dulcinea will be broken."

lash *v.* 鞭打

buttock *n.* 臀部

spell *n.* 魔法；妖术

"Oh, no! I can't do that!" cried Sancho.

"Please help me, Sancho!" begged the girl.

beg *v.* 请求

人站在她身旁。

　　男人对桑丘说："这是杜尔西内亚小姐。抽你自己的屁股3300下，这样施在杜尔西内亚身上的魔咒就会解除。"

　　"哦，不行！我可不能那么做！"桑丘叫起来。

　　"请救救我，桑丘。"姑娘恳求道。

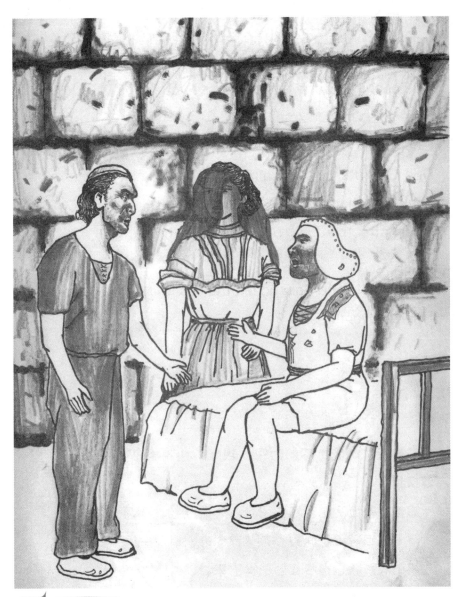

 名人名言

Once a thief, always a thief.

偷盗一次，做贼一世。

"Sancho, if you don't, I'll never see you again," said Don Quixote.

Finally Sancho started to lash himself.

Don Quixote hugged him and cried, "Thank you, thank you!"

hug *v.* 拥抱

Everyone tried hard to hide their laughter.

laughter *n.* 笑声

Don Quixote and Sancho left the castle for more adventures.

"桑丘，如果你不抽自己，我就再也不想见到你了。" 堂·吉诃德说。

最终，桑丘开始鞭打自己。

堂·吉诃德抱着他哭道："谢谢你，谢谢你！"

所有人都强忍着不让自己笑出来。

堂·吉诃德和桑丘离开城堡继续去冒险。

One morning they were walking on the seashore.

seashore *n.* 海岸

Soon a knight came riding toward them.

"I am the Knight of the Moon. I know you're Don Quixote of La Mancha. I've come here to fight you," said the knight.

"All right. I'm ready to fight," said Don Quixote.

ready *adj.* 准备好的

一天早上，他们正沿着海岸前行。

没过多久，一位骑士骑马向他们奔来。

"我是月亮骑士。我知道你是拉曼查的堂·吉诃德。我是来跟你决斗的。"骑士说。

"好啊，我随时准备战斗。"堂·吉诃德说。

"If you lose, you must go back home. If you win, all my money will be yours," said the knight.

win *v.* 赢

The fight began, but within a minute Don Quixote lay on the ground. The Knight of the Moon left without a word.

within *prep.*
在……之内

In fact, he was Don Quixote's neighbor. The village people had sent him to take Don Quixote back home.

"如果你输了，你就得滚回家去；如果你赢了，那我的钱就都归你了。"骑士说。

决斗开始了，可是堂•吉诃德一下子就倒在了地上。月亮骑士一言不发地走了。

其实，他是堂•吉诃德的邻居。是村民们派他来带堂•吉诃德回家的。

Don Quixote and Sancho had to go home.

Finally they arrived at their home village.

"I'm tired of the adventure," Don Quixote said.

He really looked weak.

Don Quixote called his friends and Sancho and said, "I have happy news. I'm

have to 不得不

call *v.* 召集

堂•吉诃德和桑丘只得回家。

他们终于回到了自己的村庄。

"我不想再去冒险了。"堂•吉诃德说。

他看起来疲惫不堪。

堂•吉诃德把他的朋友们和桑丘叫到身边，说："我有个好消

no longer Don Quixote of La Mancha."

He said to his niece, "Be careful when you marry. Your husband must never read any books about knights. If you do not listen to me, you won't get even a penny from me." Then Don Quixote closed his eyes.

That was the end of the Knight of La

no longer 不再	
marry *v.* 结婚	
penny *n.* 分；分文	

息，我不再是拉曼查的堂·吉诃德了。"

他对外甥女说："结婚的时候要小心啊，可不能让你丈夫看什么关于骑士的书。如果你不听我的，我就一分钱也不留给你。"然后，堂·吉诃德闭上了双眼。

拉曼查的骑士的故事就这么结束了。

名人名言

Once bitten, twice shy.

一朝被蛇咬，十年怕井绳。

Mancha.

Don Quixote's friends and neighbors were very sad.

His niece and Sancho cried loudly.

loudly *adv.* 大声地

One of his friends put the following lines on his tomb:

following *adj.* 下面的

A brave gentleman lies here.

He was not afraid of anything all his life.

~~~~~~

堂·吉诃德的朋友们和邻居们都非常难过。

他的外甥女和桑丘号啕大哭起来。

他的一位朋友在他的墓碑上写下了如下诗行：

一位勇敢的骑士长眠于此。

他一生无所畏惧。

Even death could not make him weak.

At the last moment of his life.

He did not care much for the world.　　care *v.* 关心

And the world was scared of his

adventures.

He lived as a crazy man.　　crazy *adj.* 疯狂的

But at last he died in his senses.　　senses *n.* 理智

在他人生最后的时刻，

就算死亡也没能削弱他的力量。

他没有为世界留下丰功伟绩，

但世界为他的壮举而震撼。

他生为疯癫之人，

却死为理智之魂。

Anne of Green Gables

绿山墙的安妮

A Surprise Girl

Matthew Cuthbert arrived at the train station. But the place was quiet and there was no sign of any train.

station *n.* 站

sign *n.* 迹象

"Am I too early?" he said to himself.

Then the stationmaster came to him and said, "The train has just left, Mr. Cuthbert. And a little girl is waiting for you."

stationmaster *n.* 站长

令人意外的女孩

马修·卡思伯特来到火车站。可是这里静悄悄的，没有任何火车的踪影。

"我来得太早了吗?"他自言自语道。

这时，站长走过来，对他说："火车刚开走，卡思伯特先生。有一个小姑娘正在等您。"

"I came here for a boy, not a girl," Matthew said in surprise.

"I have no idea. Well, this is the girl," the stationmaster said.

Matthew turned and saw the little girl.

turn *v.* 转身

The girl was about eleven with a small, freckled face.

freckled *adj.*

Her hair was red in long plaits.

长有雀斑的

"Are you Mr. Cuthbert of Green Gables?

"我是来接一个小男孩的，不是小姑娘。"马修吃惊地说。

"我也不清楚。呃，这就是那个小姑娘。"站长说。

马修转过身，看见了那个小姑娘。

女孩大约11岁，小小的脸上长着雀斑。

她的头发是红色的，扎成长长的辫子。

"您是绿山墙的卡思伯特先生吗？我很高兴能跟您一起生

I'm very happy to live with you," she said excitedly.

excitedly *adv.* 兴奋地

Matthew, a shy and quiet man, didn't know what to say. How could he tell her he didn't want her? What would his sister, Manila say?

shy *adj.* 害羞的

"Uh... Well, let's go home anyway," he said.

anyway *adv.* 无论如何

He took the girl to his cart and drove

活。”她激动地说道。

马修是个内向安静的人，他不知道该说些什么。他怎么能告诉她说自己不想要她呢?他的妹妹玛丽拉会说什么呢?

“呃……好吧，不管怎样咱们回家吧。”他说。

他把女孩拉上马车，驾车回家。

home.

"When I was a baby, my parents died. I've had to work hard, but I've always been poor. But I like to imagine beautiful things. It makes me happy."

The little girl talked and talked. Matthew just smiled at her.

Marila was waiting for them at the door.

parent *n.* 双亲

imagine *v.* 想象

wait for 等待

"我很小的时候，爸爸妈妈就去世了。我不得不努力干活，可我一直都很穷。但是我喜欢幻想漂亮的东西，这能让我高兴起来。"

小女孩不停地说啊说，马修只是冲她笑笑。

玛丽拉在门口等着他们。

Anne came up to Marilla with a smile, but Marilla cried, "Matthew, who is she? Where's the boy?"

"They sent a girl, not a boy," he said unhappily.

Suddenly the girl began to cry. "You don't want me because I'm not a boy! Nobody ever wanted me," the girl sobbed.

come up 走到跟前

unhappily *adv.*
不高兴地

nobody *pron.* 没有人

安妮微笑着走向玛丽拉，可是玛丽拉却叫道："马修，她是谁？那个男孩在哪儿？"

"他们送来一个女孩，不是男孩。"马修发愁地说。

女孩突然哭了起来。"你们不想要我，因为我不是男孩！从来没有人想要我。"女孩哭着说。

 名人名言

One boy is a boy, two boys half a boy, three boys no boy.

　　一个和尚挑水喝，两个和尚抬水喝，三个和尚没水喝。

"Oh, don't cry. You can stay here, but just for tonight. What's your name?" asked Marilla.

The girl stopped crying and said, "My real name is Anne Shirley. But I like to be called Cordelia. Isn't it a romantic name?"

romantic *adj.* 浪漫的

Marilla looked at Anne and sighed.

sigh *v.* 叹气

When Anne went to bed, Manila said

"噢，别哭了。你可以待在这里，但只是今天晚上。你叫什么名字？"玛丽拉问。

女孩止住哭声，说："我真正的名字叫安妮·雪莉。可是我喜欢被叫作科迪莉亚。这名字很浪漫，不是吗？"

玛丽拉看着安妮，叹了口气。

安妮上床睡觉后，玛丽拉对她哥哥说："我们需要一个男孩。

to her brother, "We need a boy. The boy can help you with your work. We must send her back tomorrow."

"Marilla, she is nice," said Matthew.

"So do you want to keep her?" asked Marilla.

"Well, we can do some good for her. She has been very unhappy up to now," said Matthew.

need *v.* 需要

keep *v.* 抚养

男孩可以帮你干活儿。明天我们必须把她送回去。"

"玛丽拉，她挺好的。"马修说。

"那么你想把她留下来吗？"玛丽拉严厉地问。

"唔，我们可以帮帮她。她到现在一直都很不幸。"马修说。

"But we don't need a girl!" said Marilla.

"You're right, but perhaps she needs us. And she can help you with the housework. I can get a boy from the village," he said.

perhaps *adv.* 也许

housework *n.* 家务

Marilla thought for a while and said, "Okay, she can stay."

while *n.* （一段）时间

Matthew smiled and said, "We should be kind to her. I think she needs a lot of

"可是我们不需要女孩！"玛丽拉说。

"你说得对，不过也许她需要我们。而且她可以帮你做家务啊。我可以从村里找个男孩帮我干活儿。"他说道。

玛丽拉想了一会儿，然后说："好吧，她可以留下来。"

马修笑着说："我们得好好待她。我想这孩子太需要人疼爱

WORLD-FAMOUS MASTERPIECES Ⅰ

love."

The next morning Anne sat up in bed.

A flood of sunshine poured into the room.

She slowly looked around the room.

"Where am I now? Oh, I'm at Green Gables! This is a beautiful place. I really want to live here," she sadly said to herself.

sunshine *n.* 阳光	
look around 环顾四周	
place *n.* 地方	

～～～～～～～～～～～～～～～～～～～～～～～～～～

了。"

第二天早上，安妮从床上坐起来。

大片的阳光泻入房间。

她慢慢地环视四周。

"我现在在哪儿？噢，我在绿山墙！这儿是个美丽的地方。我真想在这里住下去。"她难过地想。

At the breakfast table, Marilla said to Anne, "Matthew and I have decided to keep you. But you should promise to be a good girl."

promise *v.* 保证；承诺

Suddenly, Anne started to cry.

"Well, what's the matter?" asked Marilla.

matter *n.* 事情

"Thank you very much! I'll try to be nice and kind," sobbed Anne.

吃早饭时，玛丽拉对安妮说："马修和我决定留下你。但是你要保证做个好女孩。"

安妮突然哭了起来。

"哎，怎么了？"玛丽拉问。

"太谢谢你们了！我会努力做个好女孩的。"安妮哭着说。

名人名言

One cannot put back the clock.

时钟不能倒转。

Life at Green Gables

"Our neighbor, Mrs. Barry has a daughter your age. Her name is Diana," Marilla said to Anne.

"Diana! It's a pretty name! Is she as pretty as her name? What color is her hair? I hope she doesn't have red hair," Anne said excitedly.

hope *v.* 希望

绿山墙的生活

"我们的邻居巴里太太有个女儿，跟你一样大。她叫戴安娜。"玛丽拉对安妮说。

"戴安娜！多美的名字啊！她长得像她的名字一样美吗？她的头发是什么颜色？我希望不是红色的。"安妮兴奋地说。

"She has dark hair and she's a very nice girl," said Marilla.

dark *adj.* 黑色的

Soon Anne met Diana, and they became good friends. They had a great time together in the forest or by the river.

"Diana, I love everything at Green Gables!" exclaimed Anne.

everything *pron.* 一切

Avonlea School started in September.

September *n.* 九月

On the way to school, Diana said to

"她的头发是黑色的，她是个很好的姑娘。"玛丽拉说。

不久，安妮和戴安娜见面了，并且成了好朋友。她们一起在树林里和小河边快活地玩耍。

"戴安娜，我爱绿山墙的一切！"安妮大声喊道。

九月，埃文利学校开学了。

在上学的路上，戴安娜对安妮说："你今天会见到吉尔伯特·

Anne, "You will meet Gilbert Blythe today.
He's a very good-looking boy."

good-looking *adj.*
好看的

"I'm not interested in boys," said Anne.

In the classroom Gilbert looked at
Anne.

classroom *n.* 教室

He wanted to talk to her but she
looked out of the window.

He pulled her red plaits and whispered,
"Carrots! Carrots!"

whisper *v.* 低声说

布莱思。他是个很帅的男孩。"

"我对男孩不感兴趣。"安妮说。

在教室里，吉尔伯特看着安妮。

他想和她说话，但是她却望着窗外。

他扯了扯她的红辫子，小声叫道："胡萝卜！胡萝卜！"

"What? You are a horrible boy!" Anne cried and threw her books at Gilbert's head.

"Anne Shirley, go and stand in front of the class," their teacher, Mr. Philips said.

Anne had to stand there for the rest of the day.

The next day some children were playing outside at lunch time. They were

horrible *adj.* 讨厌的	
in front of 在……前面	
rest *n.* 剩余部分	

"什么?你是个讨厌鬼!"安妮喊着,把书本朝吉尔伯特的脑袋扔去。

"安妮·雪莉,站在全班同学的面前。"他们的老师菲利普斯先生说。

那天余下来的时间里,安妮不得不一直站在那里。

第二天午休的时候,几个孩子在外面玩耍。下午上课他们迟到

late for the afternoon class. Anne ran into the classroom just after the teacher.

"You're late, Anne," said Mr. Philips, "you won't sit with Diana today. Go and sit next to Gilbert."

next to 挨着；在……旁边

Anne's face went white.

"What are you doing? Didn't you hear me?" asked the teacher.

hear v. 听见

了。安妮跟在菲利普斯先生的后面跑进了教室。

"你迟到了，安妮，"菲利普斯先生说，"今天你不能和戴安娜坐在一起。去坐到吉尔伯特边上吧。"

安妮的脸变白了。

"你在干什么？没听见我的话吗？"老师问。

名人名言

One eyewitness is better than ten hearsays.

百闻不如一见。

"Yes, sir," said Anne and sat down next to Gilbert.

sit down 坐下

"I hate Mr. Philips," she said over and over.

At the end of the class, Anne took all her books with her.

end *n.* 末端；结束

"What are you doing, Anne?" asked Diana.

"I'm leaving school. I will never be

leave *v.* 离开

"听见了，先生。"安妮说，然后在吉尔伯特旁边坐下。

"我讨厌菲利普斯先生。"她反反复复地念叨。

放学时，安妮带上了自己所有的课本。

"安妮，你在干吗?"戴安娜问。

"我要退学，再也不会回来了。"安妮说完就走了。

back," Anne said and went away.

"Manila, I'll never go to school," cried
Anne.

never *adv.* 永不

Marilla was so surprised that she ran
to her friend, Rachel Lynde.

"Rachel, what am I going to do with
Anne? She won't go to school."

Rachel smiled and said, "Don't worry,
Marilla. I know all about children's

worry *v.* 担心

know *v.* 知道；了解

"玛丽拉，我再也不去上学了。"安妮嚷道。

玛丽拉惊讶不已，她跑去找自己的朋友雷切尔·林德。

"雷切尔，我该拿安妮怎么办呢？她不愿意去上学了。"

雷切尔笑着说："别担心，玛丽拉。我对孩子们的一切麻烦事都了如指掌。让她在家里待一阵子吧。然后她很快就会想回去上学

problems. Let her stay at home for a while. Then she'll want to go back to school soon. I'm sure."

So Marilla allowed Anne to stay at home. Diana was the only friend for Anne during those days. Their friendship grew stronger.

One evening Anne was crying in the kitchen.

problem *n.* 问题

allow *v.* 允许

friendship *n.* 友谊

kitchen *n.* 厨房

了。我肯定。"

于是玛丽拉便让安妮留在家里。这段时间里，戴安娜是安妮唯一的朋友。她们的友情越来越深厚了。

一天晚上，安妮在厨房里哭了。

"What's the matter, Anne?" Marilla asked in surprise.

"I love Diana so much," sobbed Anne.

"So?" asked Marilla.

"I can't live without her. But what should I do when she marries? I can imagine her wedding in the church. She'll be in her long white dress. After the wedding, her husband will take her away.

wedding *n.* 婚礼

husband *n.* 丈夫

"怎么了，安妮？"玛丽拉吃惊地问。

"我太喜欢戴安娜了。"安妮哭着说。

"所以呢？"玛丽拉问。

"我的生活中不能没有她。可是如果她结婚了我该怎么办呢？我能想象出她在教堂里的婚礼。她会穿着长长的白色礼服。婚礼之后，她丈夫会把她带走。哦，我再也见不到她了！"安妮哭道。

Oh, I'll never see her again!" cried Anne.

Marilla laughed and said, "What an imaginative girl you are!"

imaginative *adj.* 富于想象力的

After a few days Anne decided to go back to school.

Troubles and Dreams

trouble *n.* 麻烦

Marila invited Mrs. Man to her tea party.

party *n.* 聚会

"Mrs. Man, Anne made this cake for

玛丽拉大笑着说："你真是个想象力丰富的小姑娘！"

几天后，安妮决定回学校上学。

麻烦与梦想

玛丽拉请曼太太来喝下午茶。

"曼太太，这是安妮为您做的蛋糕。"玛丽拉说。

名人名言

One false move may lose the game.

一着不慎，满盘皆输。

you," said Marilla.

"Oh, I must try some," said Mrs. Man.

But when she tasted the cake, she showed a very strange look.

taste *v.* 尝

show *v.* 显现；露出

"Is anything wrong?" asked Marilla. Then she ate a piece of the cake herself.

"Anne, you've put my medicine in this cake!" she cried.

medicine *n.* 药

"Oh, I didn't know that. I thought it was

"哦，我一定要尝尝。"曼太太说。

可是，她尝了一口蛋糕之后，脸上显出一种奇怪的表情。

"有什么不对劲吗？"玛丽拉问。接着，她自己也吃了一块安妮做的蛋糕。

"安妮，你把我的药放进蛋糕里了！"她大叫。

"噢，我不知道啊。我以为那是牛奶呢。"安妮哭着说。

milk," cried Anne.

"Don't cry, Anne. I'm not angry," smiled | angry *adj.* 生气的
Mrs. Man.

One evening, Anne was sobbing on her
bed.

"What happened, Anne? Why are you | happen *v.* 发生
crying?" asked Marilla.

"Oh, what should I do? Look at my | look at 看
hair," said Anne.

"别哭，安妮。我没生你的气。"曼太太笑道。

一天晚上，安妮在床上哭。

"怎么回事，安妮?你怎么哭了?"玛丽拉问。

"噢，我该怎么办啊?看我的头发。"安妮说。

Oops! Anne's red hair was now a horrible dark green.

"Anne! What have you done with your hair?" asked Marilla.

"I bought something from a man. He said it would change my hair color. How stupid I was!" Anne cried and cried.

Marilla washed Anne's hair several times but the color was still horrible.

stupid *adj.* 愚蠢的

several *det.* 一些

still *adv.* 仍然

哎呀！安妮的红头发现在变成了一种可怕的深绿色。

"安妮！你对你的头发做了什么？"玛丽拉问。

"我从一个人那里买了点儿东西。他说那东西能改变我头发的颜色。我真是太蠢了！"安妮泣不成声。

玛丽拉把安妮的头发洗了很多遍，但是它的颜色还是很恐怖。

Finally Marilla decided to cut it all off.

People were surprised at Anne's short hair. But no one knew the secret.

One day Anne and her friends were playing in an old boat.

Anne said, "Let's imagine. I'm a prisoner and I'll escape by boat. You meet me at the bridge."

The boat began to carry Anne down

cut off	剪下
secret n.	秘密
prisoner n.	罪犯

最后，玛丽拉决定把它全部剪掉。

大家看到安妮的短发时都很惊讶。但是没人知道内情。

一天，安妮和朋友们正在一条旧船上玩耍。

安妮说："让我们想象一下。我是个囚犯，我要坐船逃跑。你们和我在桥那里会合。"

船载着安妮顺流而下。这时河水从船上的一个洞中涌了进来！

the river. Then water came in through a hole in the boat! Luckily she caught a branch over the river. When poor Anne was about to fall, Gilbert came in his boat!

branch *n.* 树枝

fall *v.* 落下

"Anne, what are you doing there?" he helped her into his boat.

"Thank you for helping me," Anne said

幸运的是，她抓住了小河上方的一根树枝。当可怜的安妮就要落水的时候，吉尔伯特划船过来了！

"安妮，你在那儿干什么？"他帮她跳到他的船上。

"谢谢你帮了我。"安妮冷漠地说。

名人名言

One good turn deserves another.

行善积德。

coldly.

"Anne," he said, "I'm sorry I called you carrots. Can we forget it and be friends?"

But Anne said, "No, I shall never be your friend."

"All right. I'll never ask you again!" Gilbert said and went away.

More years passed. Anne was a high school student.

coldly *adv.* 冷淡地	
forget *v.* 忘记	
go away 离开	
pass *v.* 过去；消逝	

"安妮，"他说，"我很抱歉以前叫你'胡萝卜'。我们可以忘记那件事，交个朋友吗？"

但是安妮说："不，我永远不会做你的朋友。"

"那好。我再也不会请求你了！"吉尔伯特说完便走了。

又过了很多年。安妮是一名高中生了。

"Your Anne is a big girl now. She's taller than you," Rachel said to Marilla.

"You're right!" nodded Marilla.

nod *v.* 点头

"And she's very beautiful now. She doesn't get into any trouble these days," said Rachel.

"I can't imagine my life without her," sighed Marilla.

Later, Matthew saw his sister crying in

cry *v.* 哭泣

"你们家的安妮现在是个大姑娘了。她比你都高了。"雷切尔对玛丽拉说。

"你说的没错!"玛丽拉点头道。

"而且她现在出落得很漂亮。如今她也不闯祸了。"雷切尔说。

"我无法想象没有她的生活。"玛丽拉叹了口气,说道。

晚些时候,马修看见妹妹在厨房里哭泣。

the kitchen.

"What's the matter?" he asked.

"I was thinking about Anne. I'll miss
her when she goes away to college,"
said Marilla. "But she can come home on
the weekends," said Matthew.

"I'll still miss her," said Marilla sadly.

Anne studied hard for her examination.
If she did well, she could study at

miss *v.* 想念

college *n.* 大学

weekend *n.* 周末

examination *n.* 考试

"怎么了?" 他问。

"我在想安妮的事。等她离家去上大学时，我会想她的。" 玛
丽拉说。"但是她周末可以回家来。" 马修说。

"我还是会想她的。" 玛丽拉难过地说。

安妮很刻苦地学习，准备考试。

如果她考得好，就能上皇后学院。

Queen's College.

In June she took the important examination.

Three weeks later the news came.

Diana was the first to hear the news.

"Look, Anne! It's in the newspaper. You're first, with Gilbert, out of all the students! Oh, how wonderful!" shouted Diana.

important *adj.* 重要的

news *n.* 消息

newspaper *n.* 报纸

六月，她参加了这场重要的考试。

三个星期后，传来了考试结果的消息。

戴安娜是最先得到消息的。

"看，安妮！报纸上登了。在所有学生中，你和吉尔伯特并列第一！哦，太棒了！"戴安娜大声喊道。

Anne took the newspaper and saw her name at the top.

She could not speak even a word.

even *v.* 甚至

"I... I knew it," said Matthew with a smile.

"You've done well, Anne," said Marilla.

It was the evening before Anne left.

leave *v.* 离开

"Marilla, why are you crying?" asked Anne.

安妮拿起报纸，看见自己的名字排在首位。

她连一个字也说不出来。

"我……我就知道。"马修笑着说。

"你做得很出色，安妮。"玛丽拉说。

到了安妮临走的前一天晚上。

"玛丽拉，你为什么哭了？"安妮问。

One hour today is worth two tomorrow.

争分夺秒效率高。

"Oh, I don't know why I'm crying. You're now a beautiful young lady. You were a little girl when you came here. I'm going to be lonely without you," said Marilla.

lonely *adj.* 孤独的

Anne held Marilla in her arms. "I'm bigger and older now, but I'm still your little Anne. You and Matthew are my family, and Green Gables is my home. That'll never change," said Anne.

still *adv.* 仍然

"哦，我不知道为什么。你现在是个美丽的小姐了。你刚到这儿的时候还是个小姑娘。没有你我会孤单的。"玛丽拉说。

安妮双手环抱住玛丽拉，说："我现在长高了，也长大了，但我还是你的小安妮。你和马修是我的家人，而绿山墙是我的家。这些永远都不会变。"

Back at Green Gables

Anne was busy with examinations at the end of the college year.

be busy with 忙于

She wanted to study more at Redmond College.

"If I get the Avery Prize, Matthew and Marilla won't have to pay. I must study hard!" she said to herself.

prize *n.* 奖金

hard *adv.* 努力地

Anne was waiting for the news of the examinations.

~~~~~~

回到绿山墙

大学学年末，安妮忙着应付各门考试。

她想到雷德蒙德学院继续学习。

"如果我拿到埃弗里奖学金，马修和玛丽拉就不用为我付学费了。我一定要加油！"她想。

安妮等待着考试成绩公布。

"It's Gilbert! He's first!" someone shouted. Anne was disappointed. But then there was another shouting, "Anne Shirley's won the Avery Prize!" All the girls were around Anne.

disappointed *adj.* 失望的

"We're very proud of you, Anne," they shouted.

Anne came back to Green Gables with the good news.

come back 回来

"是吉尔伯特！他得了第一名！"有人喊道。安妮很失望。可就在这时，她又听见有人喊："安妮·雪莉获得了埃弗里奖学金！"所有女孩都围在安妮身边。

"我们真为你骄傲，安妮。"她们欢呼。

安妮带着这个好消息回到了绿山墙。

But she noticed Matthew was not well.

notice *v.* 注意

"What's wrong with Matthew?" asked Anne.

"His heart, that's the problem," said Marilla.

"Marilla, you don't look well, either," said Anne.

either *adv.* 也

"I've always had a bad headache. I must see the doctor soon. Anne, did you

headache *n.* 头痛

但是她注意到马修身体不太好。

"马修怎么了?" 安妮问。

"他的心脏有点儿问题。" 玛丽拉说。

"玛丽拉,你看起来也不太好。" 安妮说。

"我一直头疼得厉害。我得尽快去看医生。安妮,你听说了关

hear the news about the Church Bank?" asked Marilla.

"They say the bank is in big trouble," said Anne.

"That's right. And they have all our money. I think Matthew has been worried about it," said Marilla.

The next morning Matthew received a letter and read it.

bank *n.* 银行

receive *v.* 收到

于丘奇银行的事吗?"玛丽拉问。

"据说那家银行出了很大的问题。"安妮说。

"是啊,而我们所有的钱都存在那儿。我想马修很担心这件事。"玛丽拉说。

第二天早上,马修收到一封信,打开来看。

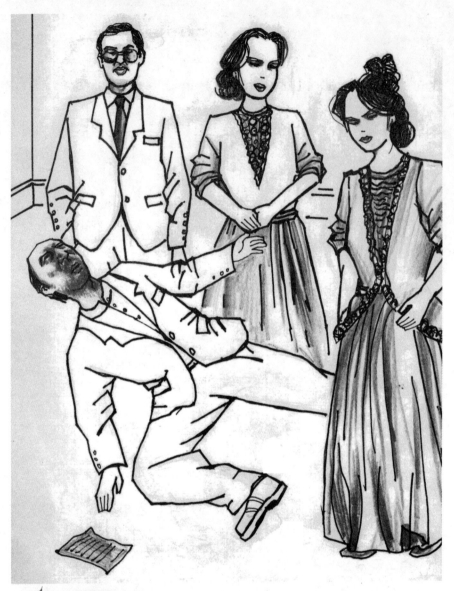

 名人名言

One man's fault is other man's lesson.

前车之鉴。

Marilla saw his face turn pale.

"Are you all right, Matthew?" she cried.

Suddenly he fell to the ground.

Anne and Marilla called the doctor, but it was too late.

Matthew died.

"It was a heart attack. Did he have any bad news?" asked the doctor.

"Yes! He got a letter!" Anne cried and

pale *adj.* 苍白的

ground *n.* 地面

heart attack
心脏病发作

玛丽拉看见他的脸一下子变得苍白。

"你还好吗，马修?"她叫道。

突然，他倒在了地上。

安妮和玛丽拉请来了医生，但是太晚了。

马修死了。

"是心脏病发作。他听到什么坏消息了吗?"医生问。

"对了!他收到了一封信!"安妮叫道，然后看了那封信。

read the letter.

"Oh, Marilla, the Church Bank had to shut down. You and Matthew have lost all your money!" Anne couldn't stop crying.

"It's no use crying. He can't come back to us again. Now we should stand by ourselves Anne," said Marilla.

One day Rachel came to Green Gables

shut down 关闭；停业

"噢，玛丽拉，丘奇银行倒闭了。你和马修的钱都没了！"安妮忍不住大哭起来。

"哭也没用。他再也不会回到我们身边了。现在我们应该靠自己支持下去，安妮。"玛丽拉说道。

一天，雷切尔来到绿山墙，她说："我听说吉尔伯特要到埃文

and said, "I heard Gilbert is going to be a

teacher at Avonlea."

hear *v.* 听说

"That's good for him. But you will go to

Redmond soon, Anne. I will miss you,"

sighed Marilla.

The next day Marilla visited the doctor.

visit *v.* 拜访；访问

"What did the doctor say?" asked

Anne.

"He said my eyes aren't well. I must

利学校当老师。"

"那真不错。但是你很快就要去雷德蒙德学院了，安妮。我会想你的。"玛丽拉叹了口气，说道。

第二天，玛丽拉去看了病。

"医生怎么说?"安妮问。

"他说我的眼睛不太好。我必须戴眼镜，这样我就不会再头疼

wear glasses and then I won't have headaches any more. But if I'm not careful, I'll be blind in six months. Anne, I can't support you any more. Oh, I must sell Green Gables," sobbed Marilla.

That night Anne thought for a long time. Then she decided what to do.

The next morning Anne said to Manila, "We must keep Green Gables because

careful *adj.* 小心的

support *v.* 养活；
      抚养

sell *v.* 卖

了。但是如果我不小心的话，六个月后我就会失明。安妮，我供养不起你了。噢，我得卖掉绿山墙。"玛丽拉哭着说。

那天晚上，安妮思量了很长时间。然后，她有了决定。

第二天早上，安妮对玛丽拉说："我们必须保住绿山墙，因为

it's our home. I'm not going to Redmond.
I think I can teach near here."

teach *v.* 教书；教授

"No! You wanted to go to Redmond so
much," cried Marilla.

"But now I want to stay with you here
at Green Gables. It's more important than
anything else," said Anne.

else *adj.* 其他的

Marilla tried not to cry but she couldn't.

After a few days, Rachel came and

它是我们的家。我不去雷德蒙德了。我想我可以在这附近教书。"

"不！你那么想去雷德蒙德上学。"玛丽拉惊呼。

"但是现在我想和你一起待在绿山墙。这比什么都重要。"
安妮说。

玛丽拉忍不住哭了。

几天后，雷切尔来看她们，她说："你们听说吉尔伯特的事了

名人名言

One never loses anything by politeness.

讲礼貌不吃亏。

said, "Did you hear of Gilbert? He won't teach at Avonlea."

"Really? Why not?" asked Anne.

really *adv.* 真的

"He heard that you wanted to stay with Marilla. So he decided to teach at another school," said Rachel.

Anne saw Gilbert walking down the hill that afternoon.

hill *n.* 小山

吗?他不会在埃文利教书了。"

"真的吗?为什么?"安妮问。

"他听说你想留下来和玛丽拉在一起。所以他决定去另一所学校教书。"雷切尔说。

那天下午,安妮看见吉尔伯特正往山下走。

He lifted his cap a little and tried to pass by Anne.

"Hello, Gilbert," said Anne softly.

He stopped and looked at her in surprise.

"I want to thank you, Gilbert. You gave up that school for me," said Anne.

He smiled and said, "I'm happy to help you, Anne. Are we going to be friends

cap *n.* 帽子	
softly *adv.* 温和地； 轻轻地	
give up 放弃	

~~~~~~

他稍稍抬了抬帽子，打算从安妮身边走过。

"你好，吉尔伯特。"安妮轻声地说。

他停下脚步，吃惊地看着她。

"我想谢谢你，吉尔伯特。你为了我放弃了在那所学校工作的机会。"安妮说。

他微微一笑，说道："我很高兴能帮到你，安妮。现在我们可

now? Can you forgive me for calling you carrots?"

"I forgave you a long time ago," Anne smiled.

The cherry blossoms were fluttering above the two young people.

flutter *v.* 飘动

above *prep.*
在……上面

以成为朋友了吗？你能原谅我曾经叫你'胡萝卜'吗？"

"我很久以前就原谅你了。"安妮笑道。

樱花在两个年轻人的上方飘扬飞舞。